Divorced But Not Defeated

DIVORCED BUT NOT DEFEATED

Woman, You Will Win After This

Marquette L. Walker

Copyright © 2024 Marquette L. Walker

All rights reserved. No part of this publication may be reproduced, distributed or transmitted in any form or by any means, including photocopying, recording, or other electronic or mechanical methods, without the prior written permission of the publisher, except in the case of brief quotations embodied in critical reviews and certain other noncommercial uses permitted by copyright law.

Although the author and publisher have made every effort to ensure that the information in this book was correct at press time, the author and publisher do not assume and hereby disclaim any liability to any party for any loss, damage, or disruption caused by errors or omissions, whether such errors or omissions result from negligence, accident, or any other cause.

Adherence to all applicable laws and regulations, including international, federal, state and local governing professional licensing, business practices, advertising, and all other aspects of doing business in the US, Canada or any other jurisdiction is the sole responsibility of the reader and consumer.

Neither the author nor the publisher assumes any responsibility or liability whatsoever on behalf of the consumer or reader of this material. Any perceived slight of any individual or organization is purely unintentional.

The resources in this book are provided for informational purposes only and should not be used to replace the specialized training and professional judgment of a health care or mental health care professional.

Neither the author nor the publisher can be held responsible for the use of the information provided within this book. Please always consult a trained professional before deciding to treat yourself or others.

ISBN: 979-8-9892806-3-6

120 PUBLISHING HOUSE
www.120dayspublishing.com

Dedications

I want to dedicate this book to my Parents. First, my mom for teaching me how to pray, trust in God, and dream big and to my dad for teaching me the work ethic to fund it all.

To my son's who help bring my story to life.

To my current husband Gabe Walker for being the vessel that God used to motivate me in this season.

To my friends that know the chapters that were left unsaid and to the ones who saw God's hand on my life before I did.

To my coaches for motivating me to stick to it when the words wouldn't come.

To my mentors who inspired me to use my story to reach women who need healing, strength, and the roadmap to winning.

To my sisters Kaytrena, Marshette, Malisha, and Shyreeta for being my sounding board and having my back when necessary.

To the reader, find your courage, strength, and dedication to yourself to release your shame, fear, and guilt and tell your story.

To myself for allowing God to put me back on the potter's wheel to reshape my destiny.

To the past that shaped me, the present that nurtures me, and the future that awaits me.

To the challenges that made me stronger and the obstacles that became stepping stones.

In loving memory of my Mom, my uncle and aunt George and Sylvia Boyd, whose stories live on in these pages.

Acknowledgements

I would like to thank my 120 Publishing House, scribes, editors, graphic designers, photographers for bringing the pages of my story to life.

To my pastor's and leaders; Pastor Scott and Tekeisha Delk for seeing me through the eyes of God and allowing me to grow/develop under your leadership.

To Mrs. Gloria for being the first to set the stage for me to tell my story.

Get Your Free Gift!

Hey Sunshine! Listen, I want you to know, you are not alone on this journey. I want to connect with you and help you overcome the stigmas behind divorce while encouraging you daily. So I have a special gift for you, an affirmation that I have prayed that has helped me. Simply click the link or visit the link below, for access to your affirming word. Speak this prayer daily and use it to take the next steps needed to win after this!

You can get a copy by visiting:
www.marquettelwalkerministries.com

Contents

Acknowledgements	vii
Preface	1
Introduction	5

CHAPTER 1
Divorced But Not Defeated — 11

CHAPTER 2
The Well of Youthful Infatuation: Divorce #1 — 15

CHAPTER 3
The Well of Familiarity: Divorce #2 — 25

CHAPTER 4
The Well of Distress- Divorce #3 — 35

CHAPTER 5
The Shame at the Well: The Stigma
of Multiple Marriages — 47

CHAPTER 6
The Well of Forgiveness With My Fathers — 59

CHAPTER 7
The Well of Preparation: Learning Me
and Letting Go — 69

CHAPTER 8
The Well of Realization - Divorce #4 — 77

CHAPTER 9
The Well of Grace: The Marriage God Gave Me — 83

Epilogue — 89
About the Author — 93

Preface

An Open Letter to Every Woman on a Journey of Self-Discovery After Her Encoutner with Divorce

Dear Sister,

Welcome to a journey like no other – a journey of self-discovery, healing, and empowerment. This book is more than just a collection of chapters; it's an open letter to you, a woman who may have faced trials, tribulations, and transformations, particularly in the realm of love and marriage.

As you turn these pages, you'll embark on a path that weaves through the complexities of relationships, the depths of personal struggles, and the heights of spiritual growth. Each chapter in this book represents not just a phase of my life but echoes the experiences of many women who have navigated the tumultuous waters of divorce and emerged stronger.

This book is designed to be more than just a read; it's an interactive experience. At the end of each chapter, you'll find "Rest Stops of Reflection" – spaces for you to pause, ponder, and internalize the lessons and insights shared. These moments of reflection are crucial, as they allow you to connect deeply with your own journey and draw parallels to your experiences.

Moreover, I've included "Prayers of Activation" in each chapter. These prayers are crafted to awaken the winner in you, to remind you that despite the challenges, heartaches, or societal stigmas, divorce did not win. It's a tool to empower and embolden you, to help you reclaim your narrative and rewrite your story with hope and determination.

This book is an invitation to explore not just my story but also your own. It's an opportunity to look at your past, present, and future through a lens of grace, understanding, and self-love. My hope is that as you journey through these pages, you'll find nuggets of wisdom that resonate, inspire, and ultimately, catalyze the transformation you seek.

Prepare to embark on a transformative journey, one where you'll discover the resilience of your spirit and the boundless grace that awaits you. Let this book be a companion as you navigate your path, a reminder that in every challenge lies an opportunity for growth and that in every ending, there's a new beginning.

With love and solidarity,

Marquette L Walker,
'The Modern Day Woman at the Well'

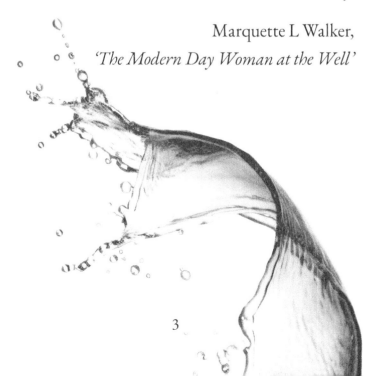

Introduction

The Plan Didn't Pan Out

In the heart of a beautiful, middle-class neighborhood, stood a brick two-story house, the kind that spoke of affluence and stability. It was the home where I grew up, the third oldest of six children, nestled in a world where the lawns were manicured and neighbors greeted each other with warm, familiar smiles. My father, a loyal Police Officer and a member of the Army National Guards, and my mother, a dedicated LPN, painted the perfect picture of the American dream.

Our home set the mold for cleanliness and elegance, each piece of furniture, each drapery, and carpet meticulously chosen by my mother, who took pride in making sure our home was ran with order and grace. But behind the façade of perfection and the strict boundaries of our 'living room' lay a deeper truth, a narrative not as pristine as the house we lived in.

Despite our seemingly perfect upbringing, with trips to grandma's, festive Christmases, and disciplined Sundays at church, there was an undercurrent of unspoken realities. My mother, the pillar of strength and the epitome of the prayerful wife, began to show signs of weariness, her once vibrant spirit dimming under the weight of burdens that were breaking up their marriage.

As a child, I watched, not fully understanding the transformation before me. My father, the superhero in my eyes, was slowly fading from the portrait of our family life. His long hours at work, his silence about his past, began to add stains to the fabric of our perfect family.

As I grew older, the truth became harder to ignore. Our move from our middle-class haven to a less familiar neighborhood was the first tangible sign of change. Our once neat and orderly home gave way to disarray, a reflection of the turmoil within. The arguments, the silent battles, the shifts in my parents' relationship – all these were markers of a reality we, as children, were shielded from.

My mother, a woman of faith and resilience, fought her battles in solitude, her prayers echoing through the walls of our home. Her fasts, her periods of withdrawal, were her armor against the pain and disillusionment she faced. It was a struggle that would later shape my own understanding of love, marriage, and resilience.

As the youngest brother arrived, our family dynamic shifted even more drastically. The foreclosure of our home, the unraveling of my parents' marriage, and the subsequent hardships we faced, all became part of my narrative. The journey from affluence to hardship, from stability to chaos, was a harsh lesson in the impermanence of life's comforts. But not before witnessing the abruptness of divorce, and shaping my own narrative of how it truly happens.loving your husband through his faults, at the cost of your value and self-acceptance then abruptly shutting it off

The love and unity that once defined us were now mixed with moments of tension, disappointment, and struggle. My mother's fight to keep us afloat, to maintain a semblance of normalcy amid the storm, was a testament to her strength. But that same level of fight was also taking an emotional and psychological toll on her value and acceptance of self love.

This journey, from a child's eyes shaped my beliefs about what it looks like to love unconditionally to the perspective of a woman who has lived, loved, and lost, is more than just a tale of a family's rise and fall. It is a story of resilience, of faith, and of the complex tapestry of human relationships. It is a narrative of learning, of understanding the depths of love, the pain of betrayal, and the power of forgiveness.

Through these pages, I invite you to walk with me as I unravel the lessons of my past, the insights gleaned from a childhood marked by both love and loss. It's a journey to understand that marriage is not just about playing roles but about the reconciliation, forgiveness, and the continuous process of building and rebuilding.

This is not just my story; it is a mirror to the lives of many who have navigated the turbulent waters of family dynamics, of marriages that didn't pan out as planned, and of finding strength in what remains. Welcome to a journey of discovery, healing, and hope..

CHAPTER 1

Divorced But Not Defeated

Sister, let me share with you a story, not just any story, but mine – a tale that zig zags through the valleys of heartbreak to the peaks of redemption. I'm here, a woman seasoned by life's trials and triumphs, standing as a testament to a journey of resilience. They call me the Modern Day woman at the well, and here's why.

As I sit across from you, on the fifth chapter of my matrimonial saga – yes, my fifth but forever marriage – I can't help but reflect on the road that led me here. It's a road paved with lessons of love, loss, and the kind of learning that only life can teach. This isn't just about the failures and victories of my love life; it's about a deeper journey, one that every woman, at some point, finds herself on.

Picture this: a young girl, eyes bright with dreams, heart full of ideals about love and marriage, nurtured in a home where appearances were paramount. That girl was me, naïve and hopeful. But, as I grew, the reality of life began to chip away at those ideals. Each marriage, each divorce, was like a wave eroding the shoreline of my dreams.

Now, why do I call myself the Modern Day woman at the well? It's simple, really. Like her, I've known public scrutiny, felt the sting of judgment. My journey through four marriages was like drawing water from different wells, each leaving me thirstier than the last. The well of youthful infatuation, the well of convenience, the well of desperation, the well of compromise – I've drawn from them all.

But, sister, here's where my story takes a turn. It was during these trials that I discovered the true essence of redemption. Each divorce, while a symbol of a dream that didn't pan out, also became a stepping stone to self-discovery. I learned that the road to truly winning in life, love, and marriage doesn't bypass the valleys of despair; it goes right through them.

In this chapter of my life, I've come to understand that being divorced doesn't mean being defeated. It's not a scarlet letter to be worn in shame but a badge of resilience, a testament to the strength that comes from facing life's toughest battles. Each failed marriage taught me more about myself, my needs, my worth, and, importantly, how to truly love and be loved.

As I stand here, in my forever marriage, I realize that the victories in love aren't about finding the perfect partner. They're about becoming the best version of yourself. It's about healing from within, understanding that the love you seek starts with the love you nurture in your own heart, and the love you allow yourself to receive from waiting and walking with God.

So, I write this to you, my sister, not just as a narration of my past but as a conversation from my heart to yours. I write as a woman who has seen the depths of despair but has also witnessed the heights of hope. If you're standing at a crossroads, wondering if your past defines your future, hear this: It doesn't.

Your journey, like mine, is unique, but the destination is the same – a place of self-love, understanding, and peace. It's a journey where being divorced becomes a chapter, not the entire story. It's where you emerge not just unscathed, but stronger, wiser, and more empowered.

In the chapters to come, I'll share with you the raw, unfiltered realities of my experiences. I'll open up about the pain, the joy, and the profound lessons learned. This isn't just my story; it's a reflection of the journey of many women. Women who have loved, lost, and found themselves in the process.

Welcome to 'Divorced But Not Defeated.' Let's walk this road together, and may our journey be one of healing, growth, and boundless love.

CHAPTER 2

The Well of Youthful Infatuation: Divorce #1

1993, a morning tinged with the crispness of fall. I stood by the window, my gaze locked on an all-too-familiar scene. There she was – my baby father's mistress, audaciously standing outside our home, and a nokia phone clasped in her hand.

"Hi, Marquette, is he there?" I remember thinking, "The nerve of this woman! To show up here? I could feel the lump in my throat start to form and hold back the angry tears that wanted to fall. My mind raced, but no words fell from my wide open mouth, as I slowly witnessed my baby's father, scratch that, my soon to be fiance', emerge from the bathroom waving his hands and motioning me not to tell her he was here. THE NERVE!

I remember slowly backing away from the window feeling empty although the baby inside my stomach was in an uproar. Before I could muster the strength to give them both a piece of my mind she was gone in her car, and I was left with him. HIM. The one who had us both thinking the other was the mistress.

The words I wanted to say were simmering inside me, but they faded as soon as I heard his voice. That voice, belonging to the man who had ensnared both me and my sister-girl with his silky web of lies. Oh, sister, we were spellbound, hypnotized by a master of deception. His words flowed as smoothly as his voice, a seductive melody that masked the chaos beneath.

His voice, effortlessly casual, borne from 28 years of life, clashed with my youthful 20-year-old tone, still raw and unseasoned. I was a product of my upbringing, a world where enduring and staying was the norm. I grew up witnessing my mother, a pillar of resilience, holding our home together, while my father ensured his mistress stayed in her lane. Yet, despite not being married to him at the time, I hadn't learned the crucial lesson of recognizing the red flags and walking away before it was too late.

What I had been taught, ingrained in me since childhood, was a simple yet profound rule: you marry the father of your children, regardless of the situation. This wasn't about romance; it was about necessity, a legacy handed down through generations like a family heirloom, albeit a tarnished one.

In hindsight, that moment marked my awakening. I realized then that the experiences of our childhood don't just stay locked within the walls of our homes. They seep into our blood, our habits, our emotional makeup. They shape our view of life, acting as guardrails that steer us, often unknowingly, along a path that mirrors those we've seen walked before us.

How It All Began

Now, let me hold your hand, walk you through my journey, not to sadden you, but to open your eyes, sister to sister. My first marriage, a leap into the unknown, was fueled by illusions of love I had pieced together from fleeting glimpses of affection and hand-holding. I didn't know any better. All I had were fragmented images, never the full picture.

That Faithful Day At the Well

The way we met seemed almost fated. My aunt and uncle's van club gatherings were a mosaic of personalities, including his stepfather. This man, with his easy charm, insisted I meet his son. At first, I was a ghost, always vanishing whenever he was due to visit. But destiny, it seems, doesn't take kindly to avoidance.

Our paths finally crossed at a club event. There he was, a vision of strength and stability, his physique a testament to his disciplined life – a football hero, a soldier. But it was more than his physical presence that drew me in. He embodied a sense of protection I had subconsciously craved, a figure of stability in my turbulent world.

But here's the heartbreak – not long after we became an item, I found out I was pregnant. # It was a twist that should have jolted me out of my reverie, but I stayed. Part of me believed that this was love – after all, isn't that what I saw growing up? The chaos, the forgiveness, the staying despite it all?

You see, the lessons we learn as children, they cling to us like shadows, guiding our steps even when we think we're walking in new light. My pregnancy was tough, a reflection of the turmoil within. I was physically unwell, constantly battling sickness, the doctors worried about my weight. But the real sickness wasn't in my body; it was in my heart, my soul, tainted by a belief that this was what love looked like.

He was there for our son's birth, a brief moment of unity amidst the chaos. We moved into an apartment, a space that felt like a haven but was just a beautifully decorated cell of my ongoing imprisonment in this cycle of toxicity.

The story continued – a repetitive loop of betrayal, reconciliation, hope, and despair. Physical fights, sweet apologies, a toxic dance that I couldn't seem to step away from. And why? Because, in some twisted way, I thought this was love. That staying, enduring, and hoping for change was what love entailed.

But here's what I want you to understand, my dear sister: Marriage is not a bandage for unhealed wounds. Your partner cannot be the savior from your past traumas. If you don't confront these shadows, they will bleed into your relationships, leaving stains too deep to clean.

I want to tell you that love is not about enduring pain. It's not about staying in a cycle that strips you of your worth, your peace, your joy. What we witness as children, the patterns we grow up seeing, they don't have to be our destiny. We can break free, we can choose differently.

It took years, countless tears, and a journey of self-discovery to understand this truth. What stays in the house doesn't always stay there. It followed me, haunted me, until I learned to confront it, to release it.

The well of youthful infatuation, left me divorced and still thirsting for real love, real peace, and a place in a man's heart that had enough room for me and only me.

Divorce Will Not Win

As we close this chapter of my life and prepare to step into the next, let's take a moment to reflect and gather strength. The journey through my first marriage, though fraught with challenges, has taught me invaluable lessons. Now, I want to share with you some guiding points that can light your path as we move forward.

1. **Acknowledge Your Worth:**

You are deserving of a love that uplifts, not one that weighs you down. Recognize your value and refuse to settle for anything less.

2. **Break the Cycle:**

The patterns we've seen and experienced in our childhood don't have to dictate our future. Make a conscious effort to break free from these cycles and create your own narrative of love and respect.

Woman to Woman: Your Winning Prayer

Dear Lord,

I come to You as a woman who has seen her share of storms. I've felt the sting of heartbreak and the weight of disappointment. But in this moment, I choose to turn my pain into power, my trials into triumph.

I ask for Your guidance as I navigate through the complexities of healing. Help me to see my worth through Your eyes, to understand that my value is not defined by my relationship status but by Your love for me.

Grant me the wisdom to learn from my past, to use my experiences not as chains that bind me, but as lessons that guide me. Heal my heart, Lord. Bind up my wounds and renew my spirit.

Give me the strength to build a loving, nurturing relationship with myself. Help me to find joy in my own company, to appreciate my strengths, and work on my weaknesses.

In moments of doubt and fear, remind me of Your unwavering presence. Let my faith in You be the beacon that guides me through the darkest nights.

I declare that I am more than a conqueror through You who loves me. I am not a victim of my circumstances, but a victor in Your kingdom. In You, I find the strength to rise above my challenges.

Lord, I trust in Your plans for me. Plans for a future filled with hope, love, and joy. Guide my steps, and lead me to the life You've designed for me, a life where peace and happiness are not just distant dreams, but everyday realities.

In Your loving name, I pray,

CHAPTER 3

The Well of Familiarity: Divorce #2

I was knee-deep in building a stable life for my boys and me, engrossed in the home-buying process, a symbol of independence and hope. My faith was my compass, guiding me with scriptures like Hebrews 11:1 and Ephesians 3:20.

The year was 2000, and there I was, proud of the progress I was making, but not recognizing the pain that had followed me. I was working hard for me and my family, so you could imagine my willingness to just get out and let my hair down, when my aunt and uncle invited me out to their event. Little did I know that would be the catalyst to me unknowingly stepping back into a cycle that mirrored my past.

Sister, let me draw you into a tale that sounds all too familiar, like an old song played on repeat. My second marriage was more than just a sequel in my life's saga; it was a haunting echo of my past. As I dove heart first into this relationship, I found myself in a déjà vu dance, one that mirrored the very steps of my previous marriage.

Picture this: I met this man, a 6'4" figure with dreads, in the very same place I had met my first husband. It was the same crowd, the same kind of event, almost as if the universe was replaying an old scene. But there was a twist – just like before, he too had another woman pregnant with his child while pursuing me. The parallels were uncanny, a pattern I was yet to recognize and understand.

There I was, focused on building a stable life for my boys and me, but simultaneously, I was stepping into a familiar trap. I was drawn to a man whose circumstances eerily mirrored those of my first husband. My journey through faith and home-buying, marked by the recitation of Hebrews 11:1 and Ephesians 3:20, was a beacon of hope amidst this repeating cycle.

But let's pause and reflect, sister. This wasn't just about the men I chose; it was about the patterns my pain introduced me to. The cycle of meeting men in similar circumstances, at similar places, was a signpost I had ignored. My mother's warnings, the subtle hints from those around me, were drowned out by the melody of familiar love songs playing in my heart.

The marriage, as expected, spiraled into a battleground of disrespect, mistrust, and emotional chaos. The first major fight, the financial struggles, the utilities being cut off – they were all chapters from a book I had read before. Yet, in this repetition, I found my moment of clarity. During a fierce altercation, I found my voice and strength, shouting, "NO! YOU WILL NOT KEEP PUTTING YOUR HANDS ON ME!" It was more than a cry of defiance; it was a realization that I was dancing to a tune that was not mine.

This relationship was a mirror reflecting not just the men I was choosing but also the unhealed parts of me that were drawing them in. It was time to recognize the patterns, to understand that the change I sought needed to start from within me. It was a call to break free from the chains of my past, to step out of the familiar dance and choreograph a new rhythm for my life.

Sister, this is not just my story. It's a lesson in recognizing the patterns that our pain can blind us to. It's about understanding that real change starts from within. If we desire a different tune in our lives, we must be willing to learn new steps, to dance to the beat of our own truth and healing.

In sharing this, my hope is to illuminate your path. To show you that recognizing these patterns is the first step towards breaking free from them. It's about realizing that for change to happen around us, it must first begin within us. You deserve to dance to a melody that celebrates your worth, respects your journey, and honors your heart.

So, to you, my dear sister, embroiled in the echoes of your own familiar dances, know that you hold the power to change the music. You are not doomed to repeat the past. You are capable of breaking the cycle, of writing a new narrative that resonates with the truth, love, and respect you deserve.

Remember, you are not just a participant in your life's dance; you are the choreographer. You can choose to step out of the familiar shadows into a new light, one that shines brightly on a path of healing, empowerment, and true love.

Divorce Didn't Win
Breaking Free from Familiar Spirits

Drawing from my own journey and the echoes of my past relationships, I hope to shed light on this intricate dance and empower you to break free from these unseen chains.

Highlights from My Journey:

- **Echoes of the Past:**
Meeting my second husband in the same place as my first was a clear indicator of a repeating cycle.

- **Ignoring Warnings:**
Disregarding advice from my mother and pastor's wife was a sign of my blind spots.

- **Financial and Emotional Turmoil:**
Similar struggles in different relationships highlighted the pattern of familiar spirits in my life.

The Power of Familiar Spirits:

1. Repeating Patterns:
Familiar spirits often manifest as recurring patterns in our relationships. For me, it was entering relationships with similar types of men, under similar circumstances. It's like being stuck in a loop, replaying the same story with different characters.

2. Unconscious Attraction:
We are often drawn to what's familiar, even if it's detrimental. This attraction is deeply rooted in our past experiences and unhealed traumas. Recognizing this can be the first step towards change.

3. Blind Spots:
Familiar spirits can create blind spots in our judgment, leading us to overlook red flags or warning signs in relationships. They thrive in the unexamined corners of our psyche.

4. Comfort in the Known:
Even when the familiar is painful, there's a strange comfort in the known. Breaking free requires stepping into the unknown, which can be intimidating but is essential for growth.

STEPS TO BREAK FREE:

1. **Acknowledge the Patterns:**
Recognize the recurring themes in your relationships. Awareness is the first step towards change.

2. **Seek Healing for Past Traumas:**
Often, our attractions are rooted in unhealed wounds. Addressing these can change the nature of our attractions.

3. **Cultivate Self-Love and Worth:**
Understanding your worth can help you avoid relationships that don't honor your value.

4. **Embrace Change and Uncertainty:**
Be willing to step out of your comfort zone. True growth often happens in unfamiliar territories.

5. **Seek Support and Counsel:**
Sometimes, an outside perspective can help you see what you've been missing. Don't hesitate to seek counseling or spiritual guidance.

Conclusion:

Breaking free from familiar spirits is not just about ending a cycle of problematic relationships. It's about a deeper transformation within yourself. It's about healing from the inside, changing the narrative, and opening yourself to new, healthier experiences in love and life. Remember, sister, you have the power to change the music of your life and dance to a rhythm that celebrates the true, empowered you.

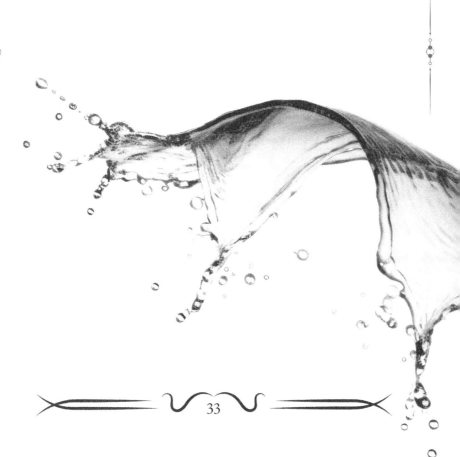

CHAPTER 4

The Well of Distress- Divorce #3

Sister, let me walk you through a season draped in sorrow, a time when grief clouded my judgment and led me down a path of vulnerability and distress. It was just days before Thanksgiving when I received the call that would forever alter my world – my mother had passed away.

Losing my mother was like losing the anchor of my soul. She was more than a parent; she was the strength, the pillar, the very glue that held our family together. In her absence, I found myself adrift, engulfed in a sea of grief that clouded my ability to see clearly. The decisions I made during this haze of sorrow were impulsive, driven more by my heart's yearning to fill the void than by reason or foresight.

Distress Leading to Rushed Decisions

In this vulnerable state, my heart, seeking comfort, led me into the arms of a man who was the antithesis of what I ever desired. He was the complete opposite of my type, yet in my moment of weakness, he became a port in the storm. He showered me with attention, gifts, and what I mistook for love. It was a classic tale of vulnerability being mistaken for readiness, of mistaking attention for genuine affection.

This man, who I had previously dismissed, became a fixture in my life. The biscuits he cooked, the comfort he offered, were but a balm to my aching heart. Yet, in hindsight, these were merely distractions, a way to avoid facing the immense pain of my loss. As I let him in, I failed to see that I was simply replacing one form of pain with another.

The Importance of Healing

What I failed to realize then, sister, is that healing cannot be rushed. It cannot be found in the arms of another or the temporary comforts of the world. True healing comes from within, from facing the depths of your sorrow and emerging stronger.

In my quest to escape the pain, I found myself *entangled* in a relationship that was a mere reflection of my inner turmoil. The more I tried to evade my grief, the deeper I sank into a situation that mirrored the chaos within me.

As our relationship progressed, his actions became erratic, disappearing without a word, only to return as if nothing had happened. Each return was a repeat of apologies and promises, a cycle I fell into repeatedly. I mistook his gestures for love, not realizing that I was merely a chapter in his book of deceit.

The Dream as a Warning:

In the midst of this chaos, I had a telling dream – a bed filled with black snakes, symbolizing betrayal and deceit. Yet, in my desire for love and stability, I chose to ignore these warnings. I was dealing with a snake, but my longing for a happy ending blinded me to the reality.

The relationship culminated in a wedding plan, a rushed affair that seemed more like an escape than a celebration. Despite the signs, despite the dreams, I walked down the aisle, only to find myself in a marriage that was nothing short of a nightmare.

The Final Awakening:

The truth of his betrayal – his true sexual orientation – was a revelation that shook me to the core. It was a betrayal of trust, of love, and of the vows we took. The moment he walked out of my life, leaving behind nothing but broken promises, was the moment I realized the depth of my mistake.

Looking back, I see now that what I mistook for comfort and connection was merely a familiar pattern of seeking validation and love from external sources. It was a cycle that only served to deepen my wounds, not heal them.

In the end, this relationship, like the biscuits he made me that temporarily filled me, left me heavier in heart and spirit. It was a stark reminder that the only way out of grief is through it, not around it.

Sister, if you find yourself in the throes of grief, I urge you to pause. Do not rush into decisions or seek solace in places that only offer temporary relief. Allow yourself the time and space to grieve, to heal, and to emerge on the other side whole and renewed. Remember, in our moments of deepest despair, we must hold fast to our faith and to the knowledge that healing comes in time, and with it, the clarity to make choices that truly honor our journey.

Divorce Didn't Win

HIGHLIGHTS AND LEARNING POINTS FROM MY EXPERIENCE

- **Vulnerability Leading to Unfitting Relationships:**
  In my grief, I found myself drawn into a relationship that mirrored my internal chaos, highlighting the importance of healing before committing to new connections.

- **Recognizing Grief's Deceptions:**
  The biscuits scenario - comfort that led to unhealthy choices - symbolizes how grief can deceive us into seeking temporary solaces that may not be beneficial in the long run.

The Overwhelming Power of Grief

- **Engulfing Emotions:**
Grief can be all-consuming, engulfing us in a tidal wave of emotions that obscure clarity and judgment. It often leaves us feeling lost and disoriented, much like wandering through a dense fog.

- **Altered Perception:**
In the depths of sorrow, our perception of what we need versus what we want can become blurred, leading to choices that may not align with our long-term wellbeing.

- **Impulsive Choices:**
Grief can lead to impulsive decisions made in an attempt to fill the void or escape the pain. These choices are often driven by the heart's yearning rather than rational thought.

- **Seeking Comfort in the Wrong Places:**
There's a tendency to seek immediate comfort, sometimes in relationships or situations that do not serve our highest good.

The Importance of Healing First

✒ Time and Reflection:

True healing requires time, reflection, and often a pause from major life decisions. It's essential to allow ourselves the space to process our emotions fully.

✒ Self-Care and Support:

Engaging in self-care and seeking support from trusted individuals or professionals can provide the necessary grounding during turbulent times.

Concluding Thoughts:

Grief, while a natural response to loss, can significantly impact our decision-making processes. It's vital to recognize and respect this powerful emotion, giving ourselves the grace to mourn and heal before making significant life changes. As you walk through your grieving journey, remember that time, patience, and self-compassion are your allies. Embrace the healing process, and trust that clarity and strength will return, guiding you towards decisions that honor your journey and lead to a fulfilling life.

A Winner's Prayer

Heavenly Father,

I come to You today, lifting up my sister who is reading this prayer. In her journey through the valleys of grief and the challenges of life-changing decisions, I ask for Your divine guidance and comfort to envelop her.

Lord, bless her with the wisdom of Proverbs 3:5-6, which tells us, "Trust in the Lord with all your heart and lean not on your own understanding; in all your ways submit to Him, and He will make your paths straight." May she lean on this promise, finding solace and direction in Your unwavering love and wisdom.

I pray for her heart, that it may be guarded and guided by Your Holy Spirit. In moments of sorrow and confusion, let her feel Your presence, bringing peace to her troubled heart. Help her to discern between the choices driven by fleeting emotions and those inspired by Your divine will.

God, grant her the strength to withstand the impulse of hasty decisions. Nurture within her a spirit of patience and reflection, so she may recognize the right path You have laid out for her. Let her not be swayed by the temporary comforts of this world but be anchored in the eternal hope You provide.

In her moments of vulnerability, wrap her in Your loving arms. Remind her that she is not alone, for You are with her, a constant source of comfort and strength. May she find courage in her faith, knowing that through You, she can navigate even the most challenging waters.

Activate in her a renewed spirit, one that seeks Your guidance in every step. Help her to embrace the healing journey, trusting that through this process, she will emerge stronger, wiser, and more aligned with Your purpose for her life.

And Lord, in her times of decision-making, let her be guided not by fear or sorrow but by the clarity and peace that only You can provide. May her decisions be a reflection of the growth and healing she experiences in Your loving care.

We thank You, God, for Your unfailing love and the promise that You are always with us, guiding us towards a future filled with hope and victory.

In Jesus' name,

Amen.

CHAPTER 5

The Shame at the Well: The Stigma of Multiple Marriages

Sister, walk with me through the maze of my life where multiple marriages painted me in shades of judgment and shame. As I stood at the crossroads of my third failed marriage, I found myself wrestling with the heavy cloak of societal scrutiny and the piercing gaze of judgment.

Dealing with Opinions and Shame

The stigma of multiple divorces was like a shadow that followed me relentlessly. It felt like living in a glass house, with every decision, every step scrutinized. The whispers, the looks, the unsolicited advice – they were constant companions in my journey. It was a world where understanding was scarce, and judgment was abundant.

I remember the days following the collapse of my third marriage, feeling the weight of the world on my shoulders. There were those who whispered that after two divorces, perhaps I was not meant for marriage. They said I should remain single, that maybe I didn't possess the essence of what it takes to sustain a marriage. These words stung, but they were a reflection of the narrow lens through which society often views personal struggles.

Facing Judgment in Sacred Spaces

As I journeyed through the aftermath of my third divorce, the echoes of whispers weren't confined to just societal corners; they resonated within the walls of my church as well. A place that was supposed to be a sanctuary became another stage for judgment and whispered conversations.

In the church, where I sought solace and spiritual healing, I found myself navigating a sea of murmurs and veiled looks. It seemed as though my failed marriages had somehow diminished my worth in the eyes of some fellow believers. Their whispers, though softly spoken, carried a weight that bore down heavily on my soul. The very place that preached love and forgiveness sometimes struggled to practice it, particularly towards a woman with a history of multiple divorces.

It was a stark reminder that even in our places of worship, human frailties and judgments can cloud the core teachings of compassion and understanding. I learned that spiritual communities are not immune to societal stigmas, and that sometimes, the most challenging battles are fought within the confines of what is supposed to be a refuge.

Navigating Corporate America with a Changing Identity

The struggle extended beyond personal life and into my professional world. In corporate America, where personal matters are often scrutinized under the guise of professionalism, dealing with divorce and name changes added another layer of complexity. Each change of name was like turning a page in a book that everyone seemed eager to read. Colleagues would sometimes inquire under the pretense of concern, but their curiosity often felt more like an invasion into a personal journey that was mine alone.

In these moments, I felt like I was walking a tightrope, balancing the personal upheavals of my life with the need to maintain a professional facade. It was a dance of masking pain with productivity, of hiding personal turmoil behind a smile and a suit.

The Path of Empowerment and Education

In seeking the possibility of sanctity in these challenges, I found my voice and my strength. I learned that while I cannot control the whispers and judgments of others, I can control my reaction to them. I began to use my experiences as tools for empowerment and education – not just for myself, but for others who might be walking a similar path. There were three ways I begin to take my power back in seasons where shame was the driving force behind my pain.

1. **Empowering Others:**
   I realized that my story could be a source of strength for other women facing judgment in their personal and professional lives. By sharing my journey, I aimed to empower them to rise above the whispers and reclaim their narrative.

2. **Educating on Compassion and Understanding:**
   I took it upon myself to educate those around me, especially in my church and workplace, about the importance of compassion and understanding. I spoke about the complexities of relationships and the journey of finding oneself amidst societal and personal expectations.

3. **Positioning as an Expert and Authority:**
   Through my experiences, I have become an advocate for women navigating the challenges of divorce and societal judgment. I created opportunities for community through actively coaching and

consulting women in ministry as well as women in corporate arenas, who understand what it's like to walk in my shoes. My voice has grown stronger, my resolve firmer, and my message clearer. I stand as a testament to resilience, a living example that one's past does not define their future.

Finding Strength in Your Truth

Amid this storm of judgment and shame, I learned the importance of standing in my truth. My journey was unique, marked by its trials and tribulations, joys and sorrows. It was a path that only I could walk, and no one else had the right to dictate its course.

I realized that while society may have its opinions, they did not define me. My experiences, though fraught with pain and disappointment, were also filled with learning and growth. They shaped me into the woman I am today – stronger, wiser, and more resilient.

My marriages, though ended, were not just tales of failure but stories of a woman who dared to love, to hope, and to try again despite the odds. Each marriage taught me more about myself, about love, and about the kind of partner I aspired to be.

As I navigated the aftermath of my third marriage, I found solace in my faith and the realization that my worth was not tied to my marital status. I embraced the journey of self-discovery, learning to appreciate my strengths and accept my vulnerabilities.

Sister, if you are walking through the shadow of judgment, know that you are not alone. Your journey is uniquely yours, and no one has the right to diminish your worth. Stand tall in your truth, use your experiences as stepping stones for growth, and remember that your value is not dictated by your marital status or the opinions of others. You are a warrior, shaped by your experiences, and your story is one of courage, resilience, and unwavering strength.

Divorce Didn't Win

Dear sister, as you walk through the chapters of your life, you may find yourself treading a path similar to mine, marked by the heartaches of divorce and the sting of judgment. In these moments, it's crucial to remember that your journey is uniquely yours. The societal whispers, the looks of pity or disdain, and the judgments that may come from the places where you sought solace and respect – none of these define your true worth.

I ENCOURAGE YOU TO TAKE HEED TO THIS ADVICE:

- **Embrace Your Personal Journey**
Your experiences, though tinged with pain, are powerful lessons that shape you. Each step you take, each decision you make, is a testament to your resilience. You are not defined by the end of a marriage; rather, you

are sculpted by the strength it took to make difficult choices for your well-being.

❧ Learn from Experience

Every challenge you face is an opportunity for growth. From the ashes of a broken relationship, you can rise with greater wisdom and insight. The journey through and after divorce can be a profound teacher, showing you the depths of your strength and the resilience of your spirit.

❧ Hold Your Head High

Remember to hold your head high. Your past is not a shadow that dims your light; it is a part of your story that adds depth to your character. Let these experiences be the fuel that propels you towards a future filled with hope, love, and fulfillment.

❧ Standing Firm in Your Truth

Your truth is your compass. It guides you through the complexities and helps you navigate the challenging terrain. Stand firm in this truth, for it is in your authenticity that you find your greatest strength and freedom.

A Winner's Prayer

Heavenly Father,

I come before You today, lifting up my sister who is journeying through the aftermath of divorce and societal judgment. Lord, wrap her in Your loving embrace and remind her of her inherent worth that shines beyond human judgment.

God, I pray that You will guide her through this time of healing and self-discovery. Grant her the wisdom to see her past not as a chain that binds her but as a lesson that enriches her soul. Help her to understand that her experiences are the building blocks of a future filled with Your blessings and promises.

In the midst of judgment, both from the world and sometimes from within, give her the strength

to stand firm in her truth. Help her to see that the opinions of others are not reflections of her value. Instill in her a spirit of resilience, that she may rise above the whispers and find solace in Your unconditional love.

Lord, bless her with the courage to embrace her journey, to learn from her past, and to step boldly into the future You have prepared for her. May she find peace in knowing that her story is far from over and that with You, she is capable of writing beautiful new chapters.

We thank You, God, for being a source of comfort, strength, and hope. May she always feel Your presence, guiding her steps and lighting her path.

In Jesus' name, we pray,

Amen.

CHAPTER 6

The Well of Forgiveness With My Fathers

The relationship with my father was always a delicate dance of respect mingled with a longing for deeper understanding. I learned that honoring your parents doesn't mean you lose your voice or your identity. It's about expressing your truth in a way that still holds a place for respect and love. Ephesians 6:2-3 says, "Honor your father and mother"—which is the first commandment with a promise— "so that it may go well with you and that you may enjoy a long life on the earth." This scripture became a guiding light, teaching me that honoring my father was not about agreement but about maintaining a stance of respect, even in disagreement.

I remember the day I hung up on my dad after an argument where he shared the same sentiments with the rest of society about my failed attempts at love. In an attempt to stand up for myself, I can admit I did the right thing, the wrong way. I saw my opportunity to bleed my truth on him, and out of anger I spewed "Have you ever considered that the flaws I brought to my marriage may have mirrored the flaws you brought to yours?"

The words I let slip from my lips and make their way to his ears, had served me so much gratification in the moment. It was like that feeling Angela Bassett had in *Waiting to Exhale*, when she was walking away from the car she lit on fire, without a care in the world.

That was me at the moment. But after the fire in my eyes and heart faded, I was still left with the aftermath of conviction. Setting my father straight and putting a blaze to our relationship, didn't change anything about my past. However it did open a door for a way for God's voice to find me in my present, and guide me into greater understanding of who He was as I walked with Him in the future.

The Fallout

The fallout with my father was not just an argument or a disagreement; it was a moment that pushed me to the edge of my emotional and spiritual boundaries. It forced me to confront the deep-seated issues that I had with parental authority, love, and acceptance. It was during this time that I realized my understanding of love was flawed.

This fracture with my earthly father became the turning point where I earnestly sought my Heavenly Father. I fell head and heart first into a relationship with Him, seeking His love and comfort. Psalms 68:5 says, "A father to the fatherless, a defender of widows, is God in his holy dwelling." In my moments of feeling fatherless, God stepped in to fill that void. He became the father figure I longed for, offering unconditional love and acceptance.

Healing and Self-Love

Through my growing relationship with God, I learned the true essence of self-love and forgiveness. I understood that to love others fully, I first had to embrace and love myself, flaws and all. 1 John 4:19, "We love because He first loved us," became a reality in my life. Recognizing God's love for me helped me to see myself through His eyes – worthy, loved, and valuable.

This has been such a pivotal teaching point for me with the women I coach and speak to in my travels. Oftentimes this is a step that is underwhelmed and overlooked in the process of truly healing after multiple marriages, and sister you need to know that there is a deeper level in trusting and loving God that will truly free you and open your heart to better. But you must first invite this type of relationship with God in, and the vulnerability of listening to what He says and obeying. I am a witness that the healing won't happen until you let Him reveal to you where exactly to start. In this season, my road to healing and self love was to start with forgiveness.

Forgiving My Father

As I drew closer to God, He gently led me to forgive my earthly father. It was a journey of understanding that my father, like all of us, was imperfect and battling his own demons. Forgiveness didn't mean forgetting or excusing his actions, but it meant freeing myself from the bitterness and pain that had held a place in my heart.

My deepening relationship with God revealed the depths of His love for me. In His love, I found healing for my past wounds and strength for my future. I learned that His love was the balm that healed the fractures of my heart and soul.

This chapter of my life brought me full circle – from pain to healing, from resentment to forgiveness, and from seeking love to understanding it in its purest form. It taught me that our earthly relationships are often reflections of our spiritual and emotional states. Healing and loving myself meant that I could now understand and accept the love of my Heavenly Father in its truest form.

Divorce Didn't Win

Sister, if you're navigating the complexities of parental relationships, remember that these dynamics are not just about the other person, but also about you and your journey. Respect, understanding, and boundaries are essential, but so is recognizing the role these relationships play in your spiritual and emotional growth. Lean into your relationship with God, allow His love to heal and guide you, and remember that in His love, you find the strength to forgive, to grow, and to love truly.

A Winner's Prayer

Dear Heavenly Father,

Today, I lift up my sister who is reading this prayer, a woman walking a path filled with challenges and triumphs, just as I have. Lord, I ask that You envelop her in Your love and grace, guiding her through her unique journey of healing and self-discovery.

Father, bless her with the wisdom to navigate her relationships, especially those with her parents. Teach her how to honor them while maintaining her own voice and identity. Let Ephesians 6:2-3 resonate in her heart, reminding her of the balance between respect and self-expression.

In times of disagreement or fallout, Lord, I pray for Your peace to reign in her heart. Help her to see these moments not as irreparable

fractures but as opportunities for growth and understanding. Grant her the courage to stand firm in her truth, even when it's difficult.

Lord, I pray that if she feels a void or hurt from her earthly relationships, You step in as the loving Father You are. Show her Your unconditional love, the kind that heals wounds and fills gaps. Let her know that in Your eyes, she is precious, worthy, and never alone.

Guide her towards forgiveness, Lord. Not just forgiving others, but also forgiving herself. Help her to release any bitterness or pain, and to embrace the freedom that comes with forgiveness. As she draws closer to You, let her experience the healing balm of Your love, transforming her pain into strength.

Strengthen her relationship with You, Father. Let her find solace in Your presence, understanding in Your words, and joy in Your love. As she grows in her spiritual journey, may she find the true essence of love and self-worth.

Most of all, Lord, remind her that she is a winning woman. Her journey, with all its ups and downs, is a testament to her resilience and Your grace. In every challenge, she emerges stronger, in every setback, she finds Your guidance, and in every victory, she sees Your hand.

Thank you, Lord, for being her constant companion, her guide, and her strength. May she always feel Your presence, walking beside her in every step of her journey.

In Jesus' Name,

Amen.

CHAPTER 7

The Well of Preparation: Learning Me and Letting Go

In the journey of life, especially after the tumultuous waves of my third divorce, I made a conscious decision to embrace solitude until God presented me with the right companion. It was a period of introspection, healing, and preparation for a love that would not be tainted by the scars of my past.

Embracing Forgiveness

The most significant part of this journey was learning the art of forgiveness, particularly self-forgiveness. It's easy to get trapped in a cycle of self-blame and regret, but I learned that forgiving myself was essential for my growth and healing. It was a process that involved acknowledging my mistakes, understanding the reasons behind my decisions, and granting myself the grace I would offer to others.

Forgiving myself was not a sign of weakness, but of strength and maturity. It was a recognition that while I cannot change the past, I can influence my future. This act of self-forgiveness opened up new avenues of peace and self-acceptance, allowing me to move forward with a lighter heart and a clearer mind.

The Power of Letting Go

Holding onto anger, resentment, and hurt from past relationships was like carrying a heavy burden that hindered my journey. Letting go was not about erasing the past or forgetting the pain; it was about freeing myself from its hold. It involved acknowledging the hurt, but choosing not to let it control my life.

As I embarked on this road to forgiveness, I realized the immense power it had to transform my life. It was like shedding unnecessary weight that I had carried for far too long. This liberation was not just emotional, but also spiritual, allowing me to align more closely with God's plan for me.

Preparing for New Beginnings

In my period of solitude, I focused on healing and preparing myself for the love that God had in store for me. I immersed myself in personal development, seeking to understand the patterns that had led to my previous marital failures. I dedicated time to grow spiritually, seeking God's guidance in every aspect of my life.

This time was not about waiting passively but actively preparing for a future where I could enter a relationship whole, healed, and ready to love fully and healthily. It was about ensuring that I wouldn't bleed old wounds into a new relationship.

Divorce Didn't Win

To you, my sister, walking a similar path: Don't give up on love, but don't rush into it either. Take this time to heal, to understand yourself better, and to prepare for the love you deserve. Remember, your past experiences don't define your worth or your future. God has a plan for you, and it's filled with hope, love, and joy.

Use this period to build a stronger, more loving relationship with yourself and with God. Embrace forgiveness, not just towards others, but most importantly towards yourself. It's in this space of forgiveness and healing that you'll find the strength to move forward, ready for the beautiful opportunities that life has yet to unfold.

May you find peace in your journey of self-discovery and healing. Remember, the road to forgiveness is the path to true freedom and the beginning of a beautiful new chapter in your life.

A Winner's Prayer

Dear Lord,

I come before You today on behalf of my sister who is reading these words. You know her heart, her struggles, and the journey she has walked through. Lord, I ask that You envelop her in Your comforting and healing presence as she navigates her own path of forgiveness and new beginnings.

Father, grant her the grace to embrace forgiveness, not only towards others but towards herself. Help her understand that forgiveness is a key to unlocking the chains of the past, allowing her to step forward into the future You have lovingly prepared for her. May she find the strength to let go of any anger, resentment, or hurt that may still linger in her heart.

As she walks the road of healing, Lord, I pray that You guide her steps. Help her to see the lessons in her past experiences and use them to grow stronger and wiser. Renew her spirit, Lord, and prepare her heart for the love and blessings You have in store for her.

Remind her, Lord, that her past does not define her. Instead, it has prepared her for a future filled with hope, love, and joy. Instill in her a sense of self-worth that comes from You, and a love for herself that reflects the love You have for her.

Lord, as she waits for the love that is yet to come, I pray that she finds contentment and joy in her relationship with You. May she use this time to grow closer to You, understanding Your plans and purposes for her life.

And when the time is right, Lord, I pray that You bring into her life a love that is true, healthy, and blessed by You. A love that will honor her, cherish her, and reflect the love that You have for both of them.

Thank you, Lord, for being her constant companion, her guide, and her source of love. We trust in Your timing and Your perfect plan for her life.

In Jesus' Name,

Amen.

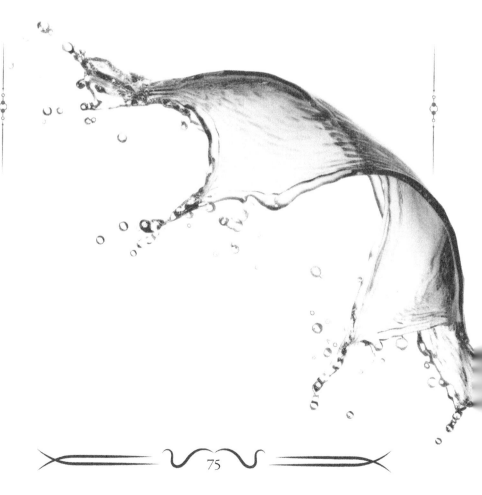

CHAPTER 8

The Well of Realization - Divorce #4

Sister, let me tell you about the chapter that unfolded with husband number four. It was 2017, and I was determined to do things differently, to do them God's way. I had learned my lessons, or so I thought, and was ready to step into a relationship where I wouldn't compromise my walk with God. I met him at work, a security officer, a man who seemed to embody maturity and strength. He was active in church, an armor bearer, no less. To me, he represented protection, a cover, possibly a provider.

We started off with casual interactions, which slowly transformed into something more. He was different, or so it appeared. We agreed to abstain from sex until marriage, a decision I was firm on. He moved in, but in separate rooms. We lived together, worked together, attended church together. It seemed like things were finally aligning.

But, sister, remember those red flags I talked about? They started showing up again. He needed attention from other women. He was still tied to his past, his ex-wife's memories haunting our present. And then, there was the age revelation - he was 60. I tried to overlook it, but doubts crept in.

Our relationship progressed to an engagement, and then to marriage. The wedding was grand, a spectacle that left people talking. But the cracks were already showing. Our honeymoon in the Virgin Islands, which should have been blissful, was overshadowed by a startling revelation - our marriage remained unconsummated.

I started questioning everything - my desirability, his fidelity, his sexuality. Was I undesirable? Was there someone else? My mind was a battlefield of doubts and fears. I turned to God, seeking answers, fasting for 28 days. And God revealed to me - his heart was with his ex-wife.

The realization hit me like a ton of bricks. I confronted him, and the truth spilled out. The man I married, the man I thought was my protector, was still in love with his past. I had to let him go. The divorce was inevitable, and it was a painful yet necessary end.

Sister, this journey taught me harsh but valuable lessons. I learned that appearances can be deceiving. Just because a man is in church and portrays himself as God-fearing, doesn't mean he is free from past attachments or personal demons. It's crucial to see beyond the surface, to understand the true nature of a person.

I learned to stop dragging the bags of disappointment and shame into every relationship. Each experience, each marriage, was a classroom, and I was the student, slowly but surely learning. When God says it's time up, it's time to listen, regardless of what others might say. My life, my mental health, was at stake.

This chapter, sister, is a cautionary tale. It's a reminder to look deeper, to trust God's timing, and to recognize when it's time to walk away. It's about understanding that self-love and God's love are the bedrocks upon which a healthy relationship must be built. And it's about realizing that sometimes, the hardest lessons are the ones that prepare us for the greatest blessings.

As I closed this chapter, I stood at the well of my life, drawing from its depths the wisdom to move forward, to heal, and to prepare for whatever God had in store for me next. In the aftermath of my fourth divorce, I realized I had been coming to the well, not just for God's love, but seeking validation and fulfillment through marriage. But this time, I came to the well solely for Him, to immerse myself in His presence. I learned an invaluable lesson: when you come to God, you never leave empty-handed or deserted. He is the source of all fulfillment.

This marriage was a stark reminder that the enemy often sends a counterfeit before God's promise arrives. My fourth husband was a mere shadow, a shell of what I earnestly desired, lacking the substance to sustain the promise God had in store for me. He couldn't perform not because something was wrong with me, but because our union wasn't rooted in God's plan.

This experience was the catalyst that pushed me to embrace the love of Jesus fully – a love so profound, it reaches out to women at the well like me. Women who have been broken, who have wandered, who have searched for love in all the wrong places, only to find that the only true and unending love comes from Jesus.

I learned that the counterfeit comes to distract, to deceive, and to derail us from our true purpose. But God uses even these painful experiences for our good. He turns our trials into testimonies of His grace and His unwavering love. This marriage, though it ended in pain, taught me to recognize the false from the true, to discern God's hand in my life, and to wait patiently for His promises.

As I moved forward, I began to understand that my worth and my identity were not tied to a man or a marriage. They were rooted in Christ alone. I realized that I needed to come to the well, not just for water, but to drink deeply from the source of life Himself. To quench my thirst with His love, His word, and His presence.

This well in my life, though filled with heartache, was a necessary journey towards self-discovery and spiritual growth. It prepared me for the true love that God had in store for me – a love that would not only fulfill the desires of my heart but would align perfectly with His will for my life.

So, sister, if you find yourself at a similar crossroads, remember this: God's love is the only love that truly satisfies. He is the well that never runs dry. Come to Him, drink deeply, and you will find the strength, the peace, and the love that your heart has been searching for. Trust in His timing, for His promises are true, and His plans for you are good. Stay faithful, stay hopeful, and let His love be your guide.

CHAPTER 9

The Well of Grace: The Marriage God Gave Me

SISSSSSSS! We made it to the final well. I invite you to join me at the final well, the well of grace. This story isn't just about finding love again; it's about the grace that transforms and renews.

After my fourth divorce, I had committed to being alone until God brought me the one for me. I was doing the necessary work to heal, not to bleed the blood of trauma and past pains into my current and future relationships. I was building a great relationship with God, learning to come to the well just for me, to drink from God, to know that when I come for Him, I'll never leave empty or deserted.

My heart had been hidden within the bosom of God, and my eyes were only seeing what God would present to me. It was a wonderful place to be. The best love affair indeed. Except it wasn't an affair. This love was permanent.

Then, two years later, amidst the solitude of COVID season, I found myself participating in a Mother's Day panel at my church. Little did I know, this would lead me to my fifth husband. Our paths crossed in a series of God-orchestrated events, from a life group based on Michael Todd's 'Relationship Goals' to unexpected encounters in church. With each interaction, I saw glimpses of his heart, his dedication to service, and his love for God.

Our relationship evolved gracefully, without haste. We respected our commitment to purity and integrity, understanding the value of doing it God's way. As we journeyed together, we were intentional about not dragging the bags of our past disappointments and shames into this new relationship. We were two healed individuals, ready to embrace a new chapter with God at the center.

This relationship was different. There were no games, no hidden agendas. We were two people, deeply in love with God and each other, committed to serving Him together. We got baptized together, symbolizing a new beginning in Christ, and led a relationship life group, sharing our journey and lessons with others. It was here where God truly allowed me to see the value of my testimony as he began to train me for the season I am in now, as a speaker and coach for women in ministry, and leaders in the corporate sector to find their value amidst lost love and misplaced self worth at the hands of divorce.

This season for us at that time was absolutely a glimpse of the glory God had in store for our story, and the impact we would have together for His Kingdom.

When I tell you I love that man, and it feels good knowing that he loves me, and I know what and how I should be loved because God showed it to me; Honey that is just the tip of the iceberg!

As God began to orchestrate our courtship, I valued the way this man looked at me. He saw me and not my past. He was not ashamed to have me on his arm, and he held me with the authority of my protector and provider. Listen, I love me so Gabe Walker! This man, who I met under the most unexpected circumstances, turned out to be the Isaac of my life, not an Ishmael. He was not just another person passing through; he was a testament to God's promise and timing. As we grew closer, we made a conscious decision to serve in church together, understanding the importance of a shared spiritual journey.

We planned our wedding, a small and intimate affair, yet it was perfect in every sense, surrounded by those we cherished. It was not just a celebration of our union but a celebration of God's grace in our lives. Every step of our relationship was a testimony to the fact that when one journey ends, another beautiful one begins.

Now, as I write this, we are thriving in our marriage, continuously discovering the depths of God's love and grace. This journey has shown me the importance of self-forgiveness and letting go of the past. It has taught me to embrace every lesson learned and to open my heart to new beginnings. Our marriage has been a continuous journey of discovery, healing, and growth. We have learned to lean on God, to trust in His timing, and to embrace the love He has blessed us with.

This marriage was the setup that catapulted me to truly embrace the love of Jesus for women like me, women at the well.

So, sister, as you read this, know that your story isn't over. No matter how many times you've fallen, how many tears you've shed, there is a well of grace waiting for you. It's a place where you can find healing, restoration, and true love. Remember, when God says time's up on the old, it's because He has something new and extraordinary for you. Your life and mental health are worth more than the opinions of others. God's grace is sufficient. It covers our past and paves the way for a future filled with love, joy, and peace. Trust in His plan, for He is the God of second chances, the God who turns our mourning into dancing, and our sorrow into joy. The God who went out of His way to meet you at the well, knowing what you were leaving and going back to, and yet and still He waited for you and offered you something more.

You are more than just a woman at the well, you are a woman chosen by God, who He loves and has positioned to win no matter how many times divorce has tried to defeat you. Let this open letter to you be a testament to that!

With love and victory,

Marquette L Walker,
'The Modern Day Woman at the Well'

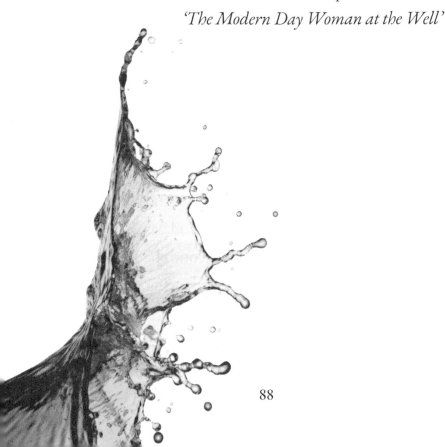

Epilogue

Drawing from the Well of Redemption

Dear sisters,

As I reflect on my life's journey, I see a profound parallel between my story and that of the Samaritan woman at the well in John 4. Like her, I encountered many trials and tribulations in my search for love and fulfillment. My story, marked by multiple marriages and divorces, echoes her quest for something more, something meaningful.

My family history revealed a pattern of broken marriages, a generational curse that seemed to have cast a shadow over us. Like the woman at the well, I found myself returning to the same place, hoping for different results. But God had other plans. He used my story, my pain, and my experiences to bring about healing and transformation, not just for me, but for those I would encounter on my journey.

The Call to Share and Heal:

Just as Jesus used the Samaritan woman's encounter to bring many to faith, God is now using me to reach out to women who have walked similar paths. My journey is a testament to the fact that divorce does not define us, nor does it defeat us. God is calling forth women in this hour to rise above their circumstances, to find healing and wholeness in Him. I have a special place in my heart for you and I want to share with you some resources that will help you on your journey on my website www.marquettelwalkerministries.com

Below, I want you to also find solace in these four concepts and the scriptures that have helped me along my journey that I share with many of my clients who are apart of my signature women who win coaching program. Your healing and redemption to life you no longer have to lead with the stigma of shame, is just a page away sis.

Healing and Redemption:

1. Seek Healing:

Your mind, heart, and soul need healing. Immerse yourself in God's Word, meditate, and journal. Find solace in Psalms and let the scriptures guide you towards inner peace.

2. Embrace Forgiveness:

Forgiveness is a gateway to freedom. It's not just about others, but also about forgiving yourself. This step is crucial in your journey to wholeness.

3. Recognize Your Worth:

Understand your value in God's eyes. You are precious, and no experience or past relationship can take that away from you. Scriptures like Psalms 139:13-15, Jeremiah 29:11, and Romans 12:2 will affirm your worth.

4. Let God Be Your 'I Am':

Whatever you need, God is. He is your Healer (Psalms 23:4, 34:18), your Deliverer (Psalms 34:17, 2 Samuel 22), your Way-maker (Matthew 19:26), and your Promise Keeper (Romans 4:21, 2 Corinthians 1:20). These scriptures were my anchors during the storms of my life.

As I close this book, my heart is filled with gratitude and hope. The well of grace is deep and never runs dry. Each of us can draw from this well, quenching our thirst for love, acceptance, and redemption. My journey has led me to my fifth marriage, a union blessed by God, where old wounds have healed, and new beginnings have blossomed.

May my story encourage you, lift you, and remind you that you are not alone. God is with you, turning your pain into purpose, your trials into testimonies. I stand with you, a woman who has drunk deeply from the well of God's grace, ready to share the living water with all who thirst.

About the Author

Marquette is an inspiring speaker, consultant, and author who brings her unique experiences and insights to your event. She specializes in empowering women, especially those who have faced challenges like divorce, by sharing her transformative journey and practical wisdom.

Hire Marquette:

The Modern Day Woman at the Well for Your Next Event, Conference, or Corporate Training

❧ TITLE:

"The Woman At the Well: Transforming Pain into Purpose"

❧ DESCRIPTION:

Ideal for conferences, spiritual retreats, and women's empowerment seminars.

Marquette explores the biblical story of the Woman at the Well and parallels it with modern-day challenges faced by women. She shares her personal journey of transformation, illustrating how to turn painful experiences into powerful lessons of growth and resilience.

❧ AUDIENCE WILL LEARN:

- Strategies to transform personal challenges into stepping stones for growth.
- Insights into self-acceptance, healing from past traumas, and spiritual growth.
- Methods to find and maintain personal peace and fulfillment.

TITLE:

"How to Lead High-Performance Women Who Have Faced Divorce"

DESCRIPTION:

Perfect for leadership workshops, corporate training, and management seminars.

Understand the unique challenges and strengths of high-performing women who have experienced divorce. Marquette offers guidance on how to support, motivate, and lead these resilient individuals effectively in the workplace.

AUDIENCE WILL LEARN:
- Key insights into the emotional and professional impacts of divorce.
- Leadership strategies for fostering a supportive and productive environment.
- Tools to empower and engage women post-divorce in their professional roles.

TITLE:
"Divorced but Not Defeated:
Overcoming Shame in the Sanctuary"

DESCRIPTION:

Suitable for church groups, spiritual gatherings, and wellness seminars.

This presentation addresses the often-taboo subject of divorce within spiritual communities. Marquette shares her journey of overcoming shame and finding grace, offering hope and encouragement to others in similar situations.

AUDIENCE WILL LEARN:-

How to cope with and rise above the stigma of divorce in faith-based communities.

- Strategies for emotional healing and spiritual growth post-divorce.
- Ways to redefine personal identity and purpose within one's faith journey.

To book Marquette for your next event
and for more information, visit:

www.marquettelwalkerministries.com

Connect with Marquette:
The Modern Day Woman at the Well – Your
source of inspiration and empowerment.

Made in the USA
Middletown, DE
03 January 2025

68221384R00064